The Meaning of Discipleship

Walking in the Way of Christ & the Apostles
Study Guide Series
Part 2, Book 9
A 9-Session Study

Peter Briggs

ISBN: 9781947642126

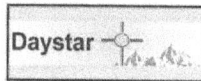

Published by:
Daystar Institute / NM, Inc.
PO Box 50567
Albuquerque, NM 87181
www.DaystarInstituteNM.us

Distributed in Africa by:
Daystar Institute/Africa
Kampala, Uganda
www.DaystarInstituteAfrica.org

TABLE OF CONTENTS

TABLE OF FIGURES

WitW
Walking in the Way of
Christ & the Apostles

Foreword

Jesus Christ, in His three-year ministry with His twelve disciples, modeled the method for teaching disciples to walk in His way.

The Walking in the Way (WitW) Study Guide Series attempts to model Christ's method of teaching by utilizing a holistic approach designed to challenge students to apply biblical principles to their lives and ministries. Our aim is to equip disciples of Jesus to "walk in him, rooted and built up in him and established in the faith, just as you were taught, abounding in thanksgiving." Colossians 2:6,7. Thus, we emphasize wholehearted discipleship, practical Christian theology, and a biblical world view.

We have prayerfully designed the WitW study materials to equip you with the tools and concepts needed to achieve this goal. May the word of God dwell in our hearts richly through faith by studying it, reflecting upon it, and allowing it to penetrate the deepest recesses of our souls. By this means, we bring our hearts and minds into alignment with God's heart and mind.

How to Use this Study Guide

Although this Bible study may be done independently, we strongly recommend using it in a group setting. Study each session prayerfully and reflect deeply on the included passages of Scripture as part of your daily devotional time with God. Establish a journal in which you record your answers to questions, as well as your reflections and notes.

If you are participating in a group study, be prepared to interact with your leader and group members. This includes sharing insights and practical lessons God is teaching you personally. Read the questions and associated Scripture passages aloud and stick to the Bible as your sole authority for answers given. At the end of each discussion

1

session, take time to pray for group member needs; then hold one another accountable for putting the lessons learned into practice.

Upon completion of one book, move on to the next book in the series. In parallel, begin sharing the WitW teaching with family members, work associates, and others in your circle of influence.

Leaders may use their discretion as to how much material to cover in any given discussion session. We also encourage Bible study teachers and leaders to read the associated WitW Theological Handbook or Theological Reader in order to gain a better understanding of the material presented in this booklet. Our resources are listed in the back of this study guide and are available on Amazon.com.

Introduction to Book 9

What is a disciple? According to the dictionary, "a disciple is a person who embraces and assists in spreading the teachings of another; an active adherent, as of a movement of philosophy." This dictionary definition helps us formulate a definition of Christian discipleship as:

A true disciple of Christ is a person who wholeheartedly embraces the Christian gospel, habitually practices it, and is persistently engaged in proclaiming and promoting it.

An important corollary of our definition above is this: a true disciple obeys the commands of his leader and King, Jesus Christ, and he patterns his behavior in accordance with the way of Christ and the apostles. From this we derive the fourth normative factor identified in Book 8; namely, **a life thrust toward Christlikeness**.

As we consider Christian discipleship, we will examine two key passages which describe the characteristics of a personality conformed to the image of Christ. Then we will explore the topic of our specific ministry identity, or the unique set of spiritual gifts, natural abilities, and interests that correspond to the good works for which each disciple is created and equipped by God in accordance with Ephesians 2:10.

Book 9 Goals

To embrace the fact that the life thrust of every disciple should be toward Christlikeness.

To reflect the Christian virtues presented by the Apostle Peter in 2 Peter 1:3-11 and the Apostle Paul in Galatians 5:22-23.

To discover your specific and distinctive ministry identity based on Ephesians 2:10.

Our desire is that every disciple of Jesus Christ be firmly rooted, built up, and established in his faith in accordance with Colossians 2:6-7. We have prayerfully designed the WitW study materials to equip you with the tools and concepts needed to achieve this goal. May the word of God dwell in our hearts richly through faith by studying it, reflecting upon it, and allowing it to penetrate the deepest recesses of our souls. By this means, we bring our hearts and minds into alignment with God's heart and mind.

As you begin each lesson, pray that God would open your heart to the study of His Word, that He would speak to you through His Word, and that He would cause His Holy Spirit to use the word of God to break up the fallow ground of your heart. This study is not about learning a lot of facts – it is about living out the truth of the Scripture in order to glorify God and impact others for the advancement of Christ's kingdom.

Chapter 1. The Beginning of Spiritual Life

When does spiritual life begin? Does it begin at birth, or at rebirth? What is its origin? How does it manifest itself in a life? These are important questions to consider.

Much of Jesus' teaching was in the form of parables – stories that illustrate important spiritual and moral principles. They are always introduced by a comparison or metaphor, whereby the spiritual concept is said to be like some physical situation with which people would be familiar. In many of these passages, the **kingdom of heaven** or the **kingdom of God** is the important spiritual concept.

Read Matthew 13:1-23, Mark 4:3-20, and Luke 8:4-15.

Q1. As you read each of the passages above, jot down your initial observations prior to answering the questions below.

Q2. Each of these passages features the Parable of the Sower, including Jesus' explanation of this parable. What is the overall spiritual concept being portrayed by the parable? What do the seed and the soil represent?

Q3. Using your knowledge of agriculture, describe what happens when a seed germinates and how that serves as a representation of the beginning of spiritual life.

John 1:12-13. But to all who did receive Him, He gave them the right to be children of God, to those who believe into His name, who were born, not of blood, or of the will of the flesh, or of the will of man, but of God. [Adapted from the HCSB]

John 3:3-8. Jesus replied, "I assure you: Unless someone is born again, he cannot see the kingdom of God." "But how can anyone be born when he is old?" Nicodemus asked Him. "Can he enter his mother's womb a second time and be born?" Jesus answered, "I assure you: Unless someone is born of water and the Spirit, he cannot enter the kingdom of God. Whatever is born of the flesh is flesh, and whatever is born of the Spirit is spirit. Do not be amazed that I told you that you must be born again. The wind blows where it pleases, and you hear its sound, but you don't know where it comes from or where it is going. So it is with everyone born of the Spirit."

Q4. In these two passages from the 1st and 3rd chapters of John's Gospel, Jesus uses a different metaphor to represent the beginning of spiritual life. What is the metaphor?

In the Parable of the Sower, Jesus employs the germination of a seed to represent the beginning of spiritual life; I designate this as the

spora metaphor, where *spora* is the Greek word for the seed that is sown. In the two passages from John's Gospel, Jesus uses human conception and birth to represent the beginning of spiritual life; I designate this as the **sperma metaphor,** where *sperma* is the Greek word for the male sperm.

Q5. Compare and contrast the spora and sperma metaphors. How do they complement and reinforce one another in their representations of the beginning of spiritual life?

Q6. What insights do these two metaphors impart regarding the nature of our new life in Christ?

Romans 10:17. So faith comes from what is heard, and what is heard comes through the message about Christ.

In Book 3 of WitW Part 1, we discussed the fact that the kind of faith that brings salvation originates outside of ourselves.

It is not our faith in Jesus Christ but His faith into us.

And so the seed that is sown and the male sperm both serve as representations of the faith of Jesus Christ. The human heart is represented by the soil and the female ovum; in both cases, necessary but passive agents in the process of new spiritual life coming into being. Note the following important principle from the sperma metaphor: the male sperm is the active agent, and the female ovum is the passive agent, both being essential; when the two are combined, the separate identities of the sperm and ovum disappear; they are combined into a new human life.

Q7. In Romans 10:17 the Apostle Paul states how the faith of Jesus Christ enters the human heart. Explain this passage in the light of the spora and sperma metaphors.

Q8. When this new life matures, what should it look like? Who should it most closely resemble, and why?

From our studies thus far, we understand that spiritual life begins at the instant when the faith of Jesus Christ is activated in the human spirit by the "message about Christ." Focusing upon the spora metaphor, this event is represented by the germination of the seed that is sown. From the seed sprouts a tender shoot which requires careful nurturing. With sunshine, water, weeding, and pruning, the plant matures and eventually bears fruit. Thus, the spora metaphor affords a rich and articulate representation of what takes place in Christian conversion.

Even as a tender new plant requires careful cultivation and protection from pests, a new follower of Jesus Christ requires one or more mature disciples to come alongside and establish him in the way of Christ and the apostles.

Both the spora and sperma metaphors serve as representations of regeneration. This is the theological term that designates the event which brings new spiritual life into being. Regeneration includes the following elements:

- The activation of the faith of Jesus Christ in the human spirit by the power-packed "message about Christ" in the hands of the Holy Spirit.

- The quickening of the human spirit so as to restore it to its proper function of connecting the human personality to the Holy Spirit. This connection is absolutely essential in that the spiritual development of the new Christ follower entirely depends upon it.

In John 3:3-8 quoted above, Jesus employs the phrases "born again," "born of water and the Spirit," and "born of the Spirit" to represent regeneration.

Q9. How would you go about establishing a new disciple in the way of Christ and the apostles?

Notes & Reflections

Chapter 2. Displaying Christian Virtues, Part 1

Just as a seed of maize that is planted and germinates in the ground will grow up to be a maize plant with ears that bear more fruit, and an egg, once fertilized, will develop into the likeness of its parents, so the seed of the faith of Jesus Christ will grow in the heart of a true believer, transforming his personality into the likeness of Christ. In fact, this is the necessary product of such faith and what is meant by a life thrust toward Christlikeness. All the apostles urged and encouraged such growth in godliness and Christian virtue. A life of righteousness, then, is not optional. If it is lacking, the professed faith is illegitimate, the enemies of God have opportunity to slander His holy name, and any fruitful ministry is forfeited.

It is essential that each disciple of Christ grow and mature in Christian character.

Peter's Seven Virtues

In 1 Peter 1:3-11, the Apostle Peter describes the character of the mature believer as one which exhibits certain moral characteristics called virtues.

2 Peter 1:3-11. His divine power has granted to us all things that pertain to life and godliness, through the true knowledge of Him who called us to His own glory and moral excellence, by which He has granted to us His precious and magnificent promises, so that through them you may become partakers of the divine nature, having escaped from the corruption that is in the world because of sinful desire. For this very reason, make every effort to supplement your faith with moral excellence, and moral excellence with experiential knowledge, and experiential knowledge with self-control, and self-control with patient endurance, and patient endurance with godliness, and godliness with brotherly kindness, and brotherly kindness with self-sacrificing love. For if these qualities are yours and are increasing, they keep you from being ineffective or unfruitful in the knowledge of our Lord Jesus Christ. For whoever lacks these qualities is so nearsighted that he is blind, having forgotten that he was cleansed from his former sins. Therefore, brothers, be all the more diligent to confirm your calling and election, for if you practice these qualities you will never fall. For in this way there will be richly provided for you an entrance into the eternal kingdom of our Lord and Savior Jesus Christ. [Adapted from the ESV]

Q1. In our focal passage quoted above, highlight each of the seven virtues identified by the Apostle Peter.

Q2. Using a different color, highlight the divine resources identified by Peter for helping us grow in our ability to manifest the seven virtues. List those resources below.

Q3. Briefly define each of the seven virtues.

- Moral excellence –

- Experiential knowledge –

- Self-control –

- Patient endurance –

- Godliness –

- Brotherly kindness –

- Self-sacrificing love –

Figure 1 portrays the seven virtues of 1 Pete 1:3-11 as a seven-pointed star. Use it as a memory tool.

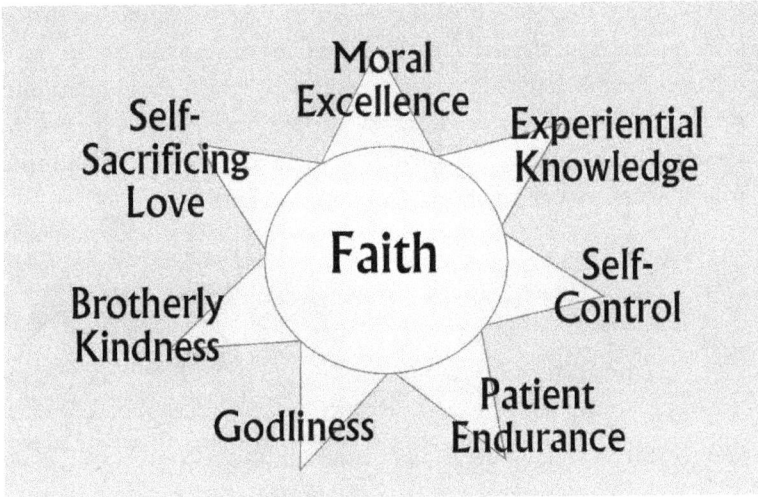

Figure 1. Peter's Star

Q4. Describe the interaction between God's work within us as partakers of his divine nature and our responsibility to supplement our faith with Peter's seven virtues.

God does not leave us without resources in our challenge to display Christ-like character. He has given us His divine power, the knowledge of His Son, and His very great and precious promises. In view of this, He requires our cooperation in developing our moral character and spiritual maturity. It is a joint venture.

The Dynamics of Peter's Star

As we discussed in Session 2 of Book 3 in WitW Part 1, the kind of faith that saves is that of Jesus Christ imparted to and activated in the spirit of a new disciple by the power-packed message about Christ in accordance with Romans 10:17. As we discussed in the previous session, the activation of the faith of Jesus in the spirit of the new disciple is the key to regeneration, by which the human spirit is quickened and restored to its proper role as the means of connecting the human personality to the Triune God. This proper role is delineated in Figure 2.

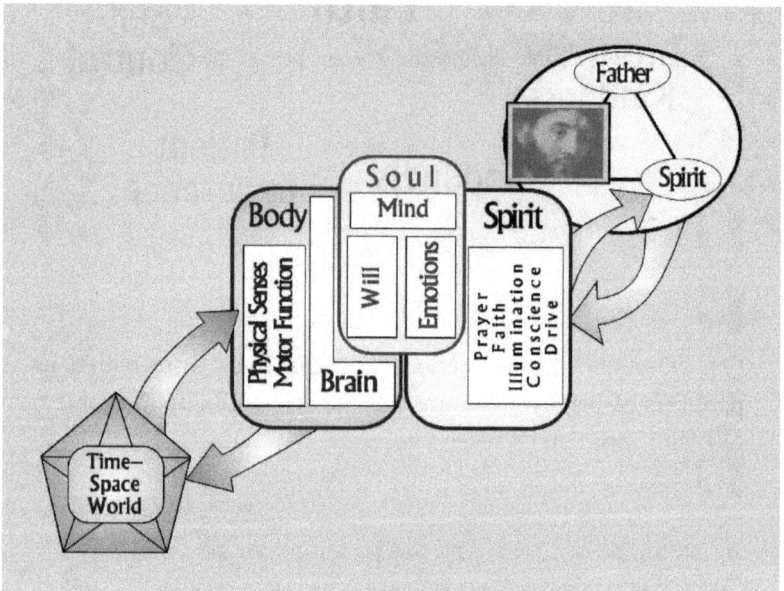

Figure 2. The Tripartite Human Personality

With that kind of faith at its core, Peter's star portrays the process of spiritual formation. Our focal text, 2 Peter 1:3-11, suggests that the Apostle has intentionally listed the seven virtues in accordance with the logical order of their development, beginning with the most

14

rudimentary – moral excellence – and ending with the most advanced – self-sacrificing love. In other words, the development of each virtue serves as the predicate for the one following. Accordingly, I visualize the spiritual formation process as a spiral with the seven virtues developing in ever-increasing magnitude over the life of the disciple.

The logically necessary product of the faith of Jesus Christ operating in the personality of the disciple is the development of the virtues of the Christian life, as set forth by the Apostle Peter.

Faith

2 Peter 1:5. For this very reason, make every effort to supplement your faith with moral excellence, and moral excellence with experiential knowledge...

Because of the central importance of faith in the process of spiritual formation and the development of Christian character, let us pause to consider several Scripture passages that define the kind of faith that brings salvation.

Read Acts 3:12-26; Romans 3:21-26, 10:17 & 12:3; Galatians 2:16-20; Ephesians 2:8-10; Philippians 3:8-9; Hebrews 11:1-6 & 11:39-12:2.

Q5. Based upon this collection of Scripture passages, write a paragraph that describes the kind of faith that saves, where comes from, and how it operates in the human personality.

Your paragraph concerning faith may have included the following elements:

15

- Faith is a means of spiritual perception.

- By means of faith we are enabled to perceive a spiritual reality in which we are immersed, but which is inaccessible to our physical senses.

- Faith is the ability to trust God.

- Faith is an act of the mind and will by which we trust, rely upon, and appropriate the gospel of salvation in Christ and its indescribable benefits.

A number of the passages listed above speak of the faith of Jesus Christ as being the basis on which we are declared righteous before God and the key to the power for actually living the Christian life. Our English translations often fail to distinguish between **our faith in Jesus** and **His faith into us**. Following are excerpts from the passages in which this is the case:

Acts 3:16. By faith in His name, His name has made this man strong, whom you see and know. So the faith that comes through Him has given him this perfect health in front of all of you...

Romans 3:21-26. ... God's righteousness has been revealed — attested by the Law and the Prophets — that is, God's righteousness through the faith of Jesus Christ, into all who believe... so that He would be righteous and declare righteous the one who has the faith of Jesus. [Adapted from the HCSB]

Romans 10:17. So faith comes from what is heard, and what is heard comes through the message about Christ

Romans 12:3. ... As God has distributed a measure of faith to each one.

Galatians 2:16-20. And we have believed into Christ Jesus so that we might be justified by the faith of Christ and not by the works of the law... And I no longer live, but Christ lives in me. The life I now live in the body, I live by the faith of the Son of God, who loved me and gave Himself for me. [Adapted from the HCSB]

Ephesians 2:8-9. For you are saved by grace through faith, and this is not from yourselves; it is God's gift – not from works, so that no one can boast.

Philippians 3:8-9. ... Not having a righteousness of my own that comes from the law, but that which comes through faith of Christ – the righteousness from God that depends on faith. [Adapted from the ESV]

Hebrews 12:2. ... Keeping our eyes on Jesus, the source and perfecter of our faith...

We take the position that it is the faith of Jesus Christ imparted to and activated in the human spirit which is the basis for justification and the key to actually living the Christian life. It is the seed that germinates and grows into a fruit-bearing plant, where the fruit consists of the virtues of Christian character and the power to perform ministry in accordance with one's ministry identity. The concept that the faith of Jesus is imparted from a source outside ourselves is confirmed in all these passages. We are impotent to contribute anything to our salvation, including faith. However, I must be quick to assert that once the faith of Jesus becomes ours, then we are responsible for exercising and developing it.

Notes & Reflections

Chapter 3. Displaying Christian Virtues – Part 2

The Seven Virtues of the Christian Life

We now return to Figure 1, the graphical delineation of the seven virtues of the Christian life listed by the Apostle Peter in 2 Peter 1:3-11.

Q1. What is the relationship between faith, the promises of God mentioned in 2 Peter 1:4, and the seven virtues of the Christian life? Identify three of the precious and magnificent promises to which Peter may be referring.

Q2. According to Peter's assertions in our focal passage, why is it important to appropriate God's precious and magnificent promises and to supplement faith with Peter's seven virtues?

Faith is the means by which we appropriate God's precious and magnificent promises – promises of deliverance from the penalty, the power, and ultimately, even the presence of evil, sin and death. Saving faith always produces a distinctive lifestyle that is characterized by devotion to God and obedience to His commandments. In fact, it is a lifestyle that displays the character of Christ.

Moral Excellence

The Greek word translated "excellence" in the 3rd verse of our focal passage is *arete* – in this case, referring to the absolute moral excellence of God Himself. Identically the same word is used in the 5th verse in reference to our moral excellence – the first virtue to be added to faith.

Q3. With the above understood, define the significance of moral excellence as it appears in the 5th verse.

Being morally excellent is closely related to being righteous. It includes the virtues of integrity, sincerity, and goodness. God Himself represents the standard of moral excellence, and our moral excellence is a derivative of His, being produced in us by the ministry of the Holy Spirit. Consider the following three passages, which describe the source of righteousness or moral excellence.

Romans 8:1-4. There is therefore now no condemnation for those who are in Christ Jesus. For the law of the Spirit of life has set you free in Christ Jesus from the law of sin and death. For God has done what the law, weakened as it was by the flesh, could not do. By sending his own Son in the likeness of sinful flesh and for sin, he condemned sin in the flesh, in order that the righteous requirement of the law might be fulfilled in us, who walk not according to the flesh but according to the Spirit. [Adapted from the ESV]

Philippians 3:9. ... And be found in Him, not having a righteousness of my own that comes from the law, but that which comes through the faith of Christ – the righteousness from God that depends on faith. [Adapted from the ESV]

20

James 3:17-19. But the wisdom from above is first pure, then peaceable, gentle, open to reason, full of mercy and good fruits, impartial and sincere. And a harvest of righteousness is sown in peace by those who make peace. [ESV].

Q4. Recognizing that our righteousness comes from Christ, and that it is essentially synonymous with moral excellence, how can we develop the virtue of moral excellence?

Because our moral excellence is dependent upon the operation of God's grace in our lives, we must willingly submit to His authority. The moral qualities of the Christian life are the fruit of submission. By willingly cooperating with the Holy Spirit of God, we join with Him in the great work of being transformed into the image of Christ and coming to share in the divine nature, as stated in 2 Peter 1:4.

Experiential Knowledge

The Greek word which is translated "knowledge" in the ESV translation of 2 Peter 1:5 is *gnosis*. While this word can designate knowledge that is scientific or theoretical, I have translated it as "experiential knowledge" in my adaptation of the ESV translation.

Q5. What kind of knowledge do you think the Apostle Peter had in mind when he wrote or dictated the 5th verse of our focal passage? What is the subject and content of the knowledge that we are to pursue with all diligence?

Q6. What is the relationship between experiential knowledge and our coming to have and to be governed by the mind of Christ in accordance with 1 Corinthians 2:16?

Q7. How will experiential knowledge change the way we perceive the material time-space world in which we live, including persons, events, circumstances, and things? How will it affect our priorities?

Experiential knowledge is derived from personal observation and experience. Peter is encouraging us to pursue with all diligence an intimate, relational knowledge of the Jesus Christ. The product of such knowledge is that we would perceive the persons, events, circumstances, and things in our material time-space world through His eyes and relate to them in accordance with His heart. It is definitely not enough for us to merely know facts about Jesus.

> *... That I may know him and the power of His resurrection, and may share His sufferings, becoming like him in His death, that by any means possible I may attain the resurrection from the dead. [Philippians 3:10-11 adapted from the ESV]*

Self-Control

The Greek word which is translated as "self-control" in 2 Peter 1:6 is *egkrateia*. In the culture of the 1st century AD, this word **designated mastery of one's sensual appetites.** Two other closely related words in the Greek New Testament are *makrothumia* and *nephalios*. *Makrothumia* literally means of long temper, or not easily angered. Accordingly, it designates **mastery of one's emotions**. *Nephalios* means to be sober or temperate – that is, not over-indulgent. Accordingly, it designates **mastery of one's appetites**, such as regarding food and alcoholic beverages.

> *These three Greek words, egkrateia, makrothumia and nephalios, convey a mosaic representation of the Christian virtue of self-control.*

Q8. Considering the meanings of the three Greek words identified above, prepare a short paragraph which describes the Christian virtue of self-control.

Self-control is the inner strength to master the emotions and physical appetites of the body. Physical appetites include eating, drinking, sexual activity, and physical activities such as work, exercise, and rest. The ultimate model of self-control is Jesus Christ Himself during His life and ministry. In accordance with His example, we are to exercise self-discipline and moderation in every dimension of our physical lives. As we mature in wisdom, we come to recognize those areas in which we are susceptible to temptation. Self-control in those areas may translate to avoidance of situations and relationships in which we may be overcome by temptation.

> *No temptation has overtaken you that is not common to mankind. But God is faithful, and He will not let you be tempted beyond your ability, but with the temptation He will also provide the way of escape, that you may be able to endure it. [1Corinthians 10:13, adapted from the ESV]*

The important passage quoted above contains the precious and magnificent promise that God will always provide a way of escape

23

from temptation. Therefore, recognizing and taking advantage of that way of escape becomes an important aspect of self-control.

In sum, we have seen that self-control is itself a multi-dimensioned virtue of the Christian life that is one of the ninefold fruit of the Holy Spirit set forth in Galatians 5:22-23.

Notes & Reflections

Chapter 4. Displaying Christian Virtues – Part 3

Patient Endurance

The Greek word translated "steadfastness" in the ESV rendering of 2 Peter 1:6 is *hypomone*. This word designates endurance that is characterized by patience, hope, and cheerfulness. Therefore, I have chosen to translate *hypomone* as patient endurance.

I quote below four passages of Scripture that illuminate the significance of the virtue of patient endurance.

Romans 5:1-5. Therefore, since we have been declared righteous by faith, we have peace with God through our Lord Jesus Christ. We have also obtained access through Him by faith into this grace in which we stand, and we rejoice in the hope of the glory of God. And not only that, but we also rejoice in our afflictions, because we know that affliction produces patient endurance, patient endurance produces proven character, and proven character produces hope. This hope will not disappoint us, because God's love has been poured out in our hearts through the Holy Spirit who was given to us.

Philippians 3:7-14. But whatever gain I had, I counted as loss for the sake of Christ. Indeed, I count everything as loss because of the surpassing worth of knowing Christ Jesus my Lord. For his sake I have suffered the loss of all things and count them as rubbish, in order that I may gain Christ and be found in Him, not having a righteousness of my own that comes from the law, but that which comes through the faith of Christ, the righteousness from God that depends on faith – that I may know Him and the power of His resurrection, and may share his sufferings, becoming like him in His death, that by any means possible I may attain the resurrection from the dead. Not that I have already obtained this or am already perfect, but I press on to make it my own, because Christ Jesus has made me His own. Brothers, I do not consider that I have made it my own. But one thing I do: forgetting what lies behind and straining forward to what lies ahead, I press on toward the goal for the prize of the upward call of God in Christ Jesus. [Adapted from the ESV]

Hebrews 6:17-20. Because God wanted to show His unchangeable purpose even more clearly to the heirs of the promise, He guaranteed it with an oath, so that through two unchangeable things, in which it is impossible for God to lie, we who have fled for refuge might have strong encouragement to seize the hope set before us. We have this hope as an anchor for our souls, safe and secure. It enters the inner sanctuary behind the curtain. Jesus has entered there on our behalf as a forerunner, because He has become a high priest forever in the order of Melchizedek.

Hebrews 12:1-2. Therefore, since we also have such a large cloud of witnesses surrounding us, let us lay aside every weight and the sin that so easily ensnares us. Let us run with patient endurance the course marked out for us, keeping our eyes on Jesus, the source and perfecter of our faith, who for the joy set before Him endured a cross and despised the shame and has sat down at the right hand of God's throne.

Q1. In the second and fourth passage quoted above, Paul uses the imagery of the marathon race to illustrate the virtue of patient endurance. Discuss the ways in which the marathon race sheds light on the significance of patient endurance.

Q2. What is the relationship between adversity and the development of the virtue of patient endurance? How was this relationship demonstrated over the course of the Apostle Paul's life and ministry?

Adversity and difficult situations are often God's tools to develop in us patient endurance. They should be regarded as something good, that we are given the privilege of sharing in the fellowship of Christ's sufferings.

The marathon runner trains hard for his race and remains focused on the prize as he runs the race with perseverance. The prize in the spiritual race we are running is that of "the upward call of God in Christ Jesus" (Philippians 3:14).

The blessings of salvation are not for those who make a one-time profession of faith, but for those who patiently endure the rigors of the Christian life and finish the course God has marked out for them.

They are the ones who overcome and will be counted worthy to share in Christ's eternal kingdom as stated in Revelation 21:7. All others will be excluded, regardless of their professions of faith and religious behavior.

Godliness

The Greek word *eusebeia* is translated as "godliness" in 2 Peter 1:6; its range of meaning includes piety, devotion, and holiness. In 2 Peter 1:4, the Apostle Peter declares that be appropriating God's precious and magnificent promises we will become partakers of the divine nature, which is the essence of godliness.

As is the case with all Christian virtues, our ultimate model is Jesus Christ Himself. His Upper Room Discourse, recorded in the 13th through 16th chapter of John, includes the following interchange between Jesus and Philip:

> **John 14:8-11**. Philip said to him, "Lord, show us the Father, and it is enough for us." Jesus said to him, "Have I been with you so long, and you still do not know Me, Philip? Whoever has seen Me has seen the Father. How can you say, 'Show us the Father'? Do you not believe that I am in the Father and the Father is in Me? The words that I say to you I do not speak on My own authority, but the Father who dwells in Me does His works. Believe Me that I am in the Father and the Father is in Me, or else believe on account of the works themselves. [Adapted from the ESV]

From this passage we can derive the ultimate expression of godliness.

The life of the godly person serves as a representation of God Himself.

Another Scripture passage that expresses the same concept concerning Jesus Christ if found in the 1st chapter of Hebrews.

> **Hebrews 1:3-4**. He is the radiance of the glory of God and the exact representation of His nature, and He upholds the universe by the word of His power. After making purification for sins, He sat down at the right hand of the Majesty on high, having become as much superior to angels as the name He has inherited is more excellent than theirs. [Adapted from the ESV]

The character of the godly person has been conformed to the image of Jesus Christ to the extent that the glory of Christ radiates through his personality.

Q3. Discuss the relationship between the sanctification process, becoming conformed to the image of Jesus Christ, and the development of the virtue of godliness?

Matthew 22:36-39. "Teacher, which is the great commandment in the Law?" And He said to him, "You shall love the Lord your God with all your heart and with all your soul and with all your mind. This is the great and first commandment. And a second is like it: You shall love your neighbor as yourself. On these two commandments depend all the Law and the Prophets." [Adapted from the ESV]

This passage in the 22nd chapter of Matthew is one of three passages in Gospels in which Jesus identifies the greatest commandment in the Torah. (See also Mark 12:28-31 and Luke 10:25-27.) From it we can derive another definition of godliness.

The ultimate expression of godliness is to love God with all one's heart, soul, and mind – that is, with the entire human personality.

Q4. Discuss the profile of the godly person. What are the aspects of his character that contribute to his being godly?

Your answer to Question #4 above may have included the following:

- Reverent devotion to God, including to love Him, fear Him, serve Him, keep His commandments, and walk in His way.

- Devotion to the word of God, including regular devotional reading, careful study, meditation, memorization, and recitation.

- Devotion to the ministry of prayer, including supplications for personal and ministry needs, intercession on behalf of others, and thanksgiving for God's answers to prayer and His daily blessings.

- A Christlike character, which serves as a representation of God.

Brotherly Kindness

The Greek word which is translated as "brotherly affection" in the ESV rendering of 2 Peter 1:7 is *philadelphia*. While the ESV translation of this word is appropriate, I have chosen "brotherly kindness" to emphasize the importance of **practice**. In other words, having feelings of brotherly affection falls short of what Peter and the other apostles had in mind. It is essential that *philadelphia* be **practiced** through acts of kindness and by being ready to forgive whenever the need may arise.

Q5. In what ways do we tend to treat family members differently from neighbors or strangers? Reflect on the level of commitment family members have for one another regarding material needs, emotional struggles, and general welfare.

Q6. Do we have the same level of commitment to the welfare of our brothers and sisters in Christ? Why or why not?

Read Acts 2:42-47 & 4:32-37.

A related concept in the Greek New Testament is represented by the word *koinonia*, which means partnership and having things in common. As we study the early chapters of the Book of Acts, we cannot help but be impressed by the incredible generosity of the members of the Christian community in Jerusalem as they freely shared their possessions to ensure that the material needs of all the disciples were adequately met. This is a powerful demonstration of *philadelphia* in action.

Read Romans 12:3-13 and 1 Corinthians 12:12-31.

The 12th chapter of Romans and of 1 Corinthians contain extended passages regarding the fact that the human body with its many members serves as a metaphor for the church as the body of Christ.

Q7. What instruction can we derive for the human body metaphor regarding the way the members of a Christian community should exercise brotherly kindness toward one another?

Read Philippians 2:1-11.

31

The 2nd chapter of Philippians opens with Paul's teaching regarding the way that members of a Christian community should represent themselves with humility in relation to the other members of the community. He then launches into a majestic exposition of Jesus' extreme act of self-emptying.

Q8. Analyze the teaching contained in the 2nd chapter of Philippians regarding our practicing the virtue of brotherly kindness.

Brotherly kindness can only be practiced out from a spirit of humility. A person who is proud may put on a show of brotherly kindness, but his motive is self-seeking – that is, he is looking after his own advancement rather than being sincerely concerned about the welfare of others.

Q9. Identify and list at least three other passages in the Christian Scriptures that contain teaching related to the virtue of brotherly kindness.

Q10. How would you summarize the attributes of a person who is practicing brotherly kindness. In other words, formulate a character profile for this Christian virtue.

The attributes you listed in your answer to Question #10 above may have included the following:

- Enjoyment of being in community.

- Mutual respect: the ability to honor others above ourselves.

- Being ready and eager to forgive in the case of an offense.

- Collaboration in the work of ministry.

- Bearing one another's burdens

Q11. Reflecting on the three virtues we have discussed in this session – patient endurance, godliness, and brotherly kindness – list action steps that God has laid upon your heart to further develop these virtues in your own life and ministry.

Notes & Reflections

Chapter 5. Displaying Christian Virtues – Part 4

Self-Sacrificing Love

The Greek word that is translated "love" in the ESV rendering of 2 Peter 1:7 is *agape*. I have chosen to translate this word as "self-sacrificing love" in the rendering of 2 Peter 1:3-11 that appears near the beginning of Session 2. Agape designates a love which is unconditional and godlike in quality; hereafter in this session I will speak of it as **agape love**.

It is noteworthy that in the Apostle Paul's list of the nine-fold fruit of the Holy Spirit in Galatians 5:22-23 he places *agape* love at the head of the list. The implication of Paul's list is that the other eight virtues are subsumed beneath and are the product of agape love.

Agape love is beyond our ability to practice on a regular basis. It is the product of the Holy Spirit's ministry within our personalities.

Other Kinds of Love

The *Koine* Greek language in which the Christian Scriptures were originally written includes two other important kinds of love in addition to agape love. *Philadelphia* designates love of brothers, or, more generally, it is the kind of love that family members have for one another. *Eros* designates sensual love. Let us reflect briefly upon these two lesser kinds of love before considering *agape* love.

Read 13th chapter of 2 Samuel.

This chapter records the overwhelming infatuation that possessed one of David's sons, Amnon, toward his sister, Tamar. I believe this is the clearest biblical example of *eros* love. The object of Amnon's *eros* love was not Tamar, but rather it was gratification of his own sexual desire. She was but an instrument that he employed to achieve his desired goal. Once his sexual desire for her was gratified, he cast her out of his sight. The 15th verse of our focal passage in the 13th chapter of 2 Samuel is most telling; after he had violated his sister sexually, Amnon hated her with an overwhelming hatred. The case of Amnon and Tamar represents an extreme form of *eros* love.

Peruse the Song of Solomon.

The Son of Solomon celebrates the love that develops between a man and his wife, which includes *eros* love.

Q1. What is the difference between the kind of eros love displayed in the story of Amnon and Tamar and that portrayed in the Song of Solomon?

Read John 21:15-19.

This passage in John's Gospel records a noteworthy conversation that took place between Jesus and the Apostle Peter during the period of 40 days after His resurrection and before His ascension. Unfortunately, most English translations of this passage obscure the significance of this conversation. Following is an adaptation of the ESV rendering that opens our understanding of what is actually taking place between Jesus and Peter.

> **John 21:15-19.** When they had finished breakfast, Jesus said to Simon Peter, "Simon, son of John, do you love Me with divine self-sacrificing love more than these?" He said to him, "Yes, Lord; you know that I love You with brotherly affection." He said to him, "Feed My lambs." He said to him a second time, "Simon, son of John, do you love Me with divine self-sacrificing love?" He said to Him, "Yes, Lord; You know that I love You with brotherly affection." He said to him, "Tend My sheep." He said to him the third time, "Simon, son of John, do you love Me with brotherly

36

affection?" Peter was grieved because He said to him the third time, "Do you love Me with brotherly affection?" and he said to Him, "Lord, You know everything; You know that I love You with brotherly affection." Jesus said to him, "Feed My sheep. Truly, truly, I say to you, when you were young, you used to dress yourself and walk wherever you wanted, but when you are old, you will stretch out your hands, and another will dress you and carry you where you do not want to go." (This He said to show by what kind of death he was to glorify God.) And after saying this He said to him, "Follow Me." [Adapted from the ESV]

In the first and second questions in the 15th and 16th verses, Jesus employs the verb form of agape love, which is agapao. In the third question in the 17th verse, Jesus employs the verb form of brotherly love, which is phileo. In all three of his responses to Jesus' questions, Peter employs phileo.

Q2. With this illumination of our focal passage in the 21st chapter of John, analyze the significance of the conversation between Jesus and Peter.

Q3. What does our focal passage in the 21st chapter of John's Gospel teach us regarding the source of agape love?

Read 13th chapter of 1 Corinthians.

This short chapter, tucked in the middle of a three-chapter trilogy on spiritual gifts and their proper use within the church community, stands as one of the most elegant and sublime literary masterpieces of all time.

Q4. Analyze the 13th chapter of 1 Corinthians and list all the attributes of *agape* love that you can discover in this passage listing what agape love is and what it is not.

The principal thrust of the 13th chapter of 1 Corinthians is that agape love is the *sine qua non* of spiritual maturity. This, in fact, corresponds to the teaching of the Apostle Peter in 2 Peter 1:3-11. Moreover, in the absence of *agape* love, all manifestations of spiritual gifts are vain and futile.

> *In fact, agape love as the motivating force behind the manifestation of spiritual gifts certifies that they are genuinely the product of the ministry of the Holy Spirit. If agape love is absent, then the manifestation of spiritual gifts, however spectacular, originates from some other source.*

Read Matthew 5:43-44; Luke 6:35; John 13:34-35 & 15:12-15; Romans 5:6-8; 1 Peter 4:8; and 1 John 3:11-12 & 4:7-12.

Q5. Summarize the teaching contained in these eight passages about the source, character, and practice of agape love.

Q6. If God went to such lengths to save us while we were His enemies, how then should we treat our enemies?

Q7. The command to love our enemies is truly counter-intuitive and counter-cultural, and to obey it in our own strength is impossible. How can we grow in *agape* love, particularly in dealing with our enemies?

Reflect on the times when you have been tempted to exhibit unloving behaviors. Is it not the case that such temptations arise in the context of difficult relationships or interpersonal conflict? It is then that we feel like being rude, impatient, or unkind.

Brotherly kindness, which we discussed toward the end of Session 4, should control how we interact with one another within the community of faith. Within that community, we have a reasonable expectation that brotherly kindness will be reciprocated. However, agape love operates at an entirely different level; it is unconditional and continues even if not reciprocated. As agape love radiates through our personalities, we are enabled to manifest the love of Christ, even when we have been wronged, insulted, persecuted, mistreated, or challenged.

Q8. Reflect on your relationships. When has agape love been called for? How did you handle the situation?

In response to Question #7 above, we discussed how we might develop in our ability to practice agape love. I believe the promise in 1 Corinthians 10:13 applies. If God invariably provides a way of escape from a temptation, then most assuredly we can trust Him to make available the strength we need to love a person who has offended, mistreated, or persecuted us. The key is to deny the fleshly response of retaliation, revenge, or holding a grudge, and allow the Holy Spirit to express the agape response, which is to bless instead of curse. As we learn to respond in this way to small offenses, God will allow us to be confronted with larger ones. By this means, we develop in our ability to manifest agape love, even to our enemies.

It is important to realize none of the Apostle Peter's seven virtues can be generated out from the energy of the flesh, and most especially agape love. It is only with the regenerating life of Christ energizing and transforming us that this kind of love can be a reality in our lives. Our job is to be willing and obedient to love this way. God's job is to work in us to do it. In fact, this is true of all seven of the virtues of Peter's Star.

Q9. Reflect on your efforts to move in the direction of godly Christian character. Briefly discuss a few of your successes and a few of your failures.

Paul's Fruit of the Spirit

Galatians 5:22-23. But the fruit of the Spirit is love, joy, peace, patience, kindness, goodness, faith, gentleness, self-control. Against such things there is no law.

The singular fruit of the Holy Spirit is the character of Jesus Christ radiating through our lives and touching the people around us. Paul represents that singular fruit in terms of nine virtues, the first of which is agape love.

Q10. What is the implication of the ordering of Paul's list of the nine-fold fruit of the Holy Spirit?

Q11. Compare Paul's list of nine virtues in Galatians 5:22-23 and Peter's list of seven virtues in 2 Peter 1:3-11. How are they complementary?

Let us reflect further on the fact that the Apostle Paul does not identify multiple fruits of the Holy Spirit, but speaks in terms of a singular, nine--fold fruit of the Holy Spirit. The follower of Christ does not bear apples, oranges, lemons, and pomegranates on the same tree. The singular fruit we bear is the likeness of Christ, which is manifested through several character traits or virtues. These are represented by the Apostle Peter in the sevenfold fruit portrayed in Figure 1, and by the Apostle Paul in the nine-fold fruit of the Holy Spirit.

God is working in us to conform us to the image of His Son, and we are called to submit to that work and cooperate with Him in it.

Our Purpose in Being

Ephesians 2:8-10. For you are saved by grace through faith, and this is not from yourselves; it is God's gift – not from works, so that no one can boast. For we are His workmanship, created in Christ Jesus for good works, which God prepared ahead of time so that we should walk in them. [Adapted from the HCSB]

According to the Apostle Paul in Ephesians 2:10, each of us as God's children has been specially created for and called to a distinctive ministry identity. Moreover, God does not keep that distinctive ministry identity a mystery. Just the opposite, He is eager to reveal it to each of us, provided we are eager to walk in and fulfill it.

42

The Christ follower must pursue with all diligence his ministry identity – that set of good works that God has prepared ahead of time for us to discover and perform. I believe that if we fail in this endeavor, there will be something in the cosmos that will be eternally unfulfilled.

Q12. Have you discovered your ministry identity? If so, what is it, and how did you go about discovering it?

God has created each of us for a specific and unique purpose within the cosmic scope of His redemptive plan for history. As each of us discover and perform that set of good works which God has prepared ahead of time, we contribute in a distinctive way to the building up of His church, the body of Christ.

Ephesians 2:19-22. So then you are no longer strangers and aliens, but you are fellow citizens with the saints and members of the household of God, built on the foundation of the apostles and prophets, Christ Jesus Himself being the cornerstone, in whom the whole structure, being joined together, grows into a holy temple in the Lord. In Him you also are being built together into a dwelling place for God by the Spirit.

Summary

It is noteworthy that the Greek word which is translated creation or workmanship in Ephesians 2:10 is *poema*, from which derive the English word "poem." Thus, each of us is a uniquely beautiful expression of the grace of God as we walk in that pattern of good works that God has prepared for us to perform in cooperation with the Holy Spirit.

The seven virtues of Christian character listed by the Apostle Peter in 2 Peter 1:3-11 are portrayed in Peter's Star, Figure 1. By means of these seven virtues the personality of Jesus radiates through our personalities and is thereby placed on display to a watching world. At the center of Peter's Star is faith – the faith of Jesus Christ that is activated in our spirits by the power-packed message about Christ in accordance with Romans 10:17. It flourishes and produces the fruit of Christian character as it is nourished by the word of God and strengthened by use. The Apostle Peter's seven virtues are: moral excellence, experiential knowledge, self-control, patient endurance, godliness, brotherly kindness, and self-sacrificial love

In Galatians 5:22-23, the Apostle Paul offers a complementary list of the fruit of the spirit: love, joy, peace, patience, kindness, goodness, faith, gentleness, self-control. The singular fruit of the spirit, then, is the manifestation of the personality of Jesus Christ.

The sanctification process in which we are presently engaged is a lifelong project in which we cooperate with the Holy Spirit in His endeavor to conform our personalities to that of Christ through the cultivation and development of the virtues of Christian character.

Notes & Reflections

Chapter 6. Discovering Your Ministry Identity

We introduced the concept of **ministry identity** toward the end of the last session as we considered our purpose in being based upon Ephesians 2:10. Because of the manner in which the Christian gospel has been proclaimed and taught for nearly two centuries, many professing Christians are unaware of the ministry identity concept. Therefore, in this session we will discuss this concept with a degree of rigor.

As I have been working through an exposition of the gospel of the kingdom of God in WitW Part 2, I have endeavored to place in evidence the fact that the object of our salvation is not simply that we might escape the torments of hell, as important as that is. Instead, we are saved in order to become functioning citizens of Christ's kingdom on earth and members of the household of God.

The function of each Christ follower is to contribute to the building up of the church, which is the body and bride of Christ. However, the way in which each of us performs that function is unique. That is, God has sovereignly conferred upon each of us a distinctive set of talents, skills, and spiritual gifts that enable us to perform a certain ministry function with great power and fruitfulness.

We designate that particular ministry function as our ministry identity.

We based our brief discussion in Session 5 on Ephesians 2:8-10, a Scripture passage which bears repeating.

Ephesians 2:8-10. For you are saved by grace through faith, and this is not from yourselves; it is God's gift – not from works, so that no one can boast. For we are His workmanship, created in Christ Jesus for good works, which God prepared ahead of time so that we should walk in them. [Adapted from the HCSB]

A Work of Art

In Session 5 I drew attention to the fact that the Greek word translated "workmanship" in this passage is *poema*, from which the English word "poem" is derived. The sense of *poema* is not only that we have been created by God, but that each of us is a **work of art** in which He takes pleasure, especially as we perform the good works that He has prepared ahead of time – that is, as we contribute to the building up of the body of Christ according to our ministry identity.

Therefore, it is critical that each of us discovers our ministry identity. I suggest that there are aspects of God's cosmic plan which will be eternally unfulfilled if we fail in this endeavor.

The discussion points that follow address first the content of the ministry identity concept and why it is important. Then we will turn to the question as to how each of us can discover our distinctive ministry identity.

Building Up the Body of Christ

The primary teaching passage about building up the body of Christ is found in the 4th chapter of Ephesians.

Read Ephesians 4:7-16.

Q1. What has God given the church to enable the process of building up the body of Christ?

Q2. Who is to perform the works of ministry to effect or actualize the building up of the body of Christ?

Q3. How does the Apostle Paul represent the goal of the project of building up of the body Christ?

The Employment of Spiritual Gifts

The primary teaching passages on the employment of spiritual gifts for the building up of the body of Christ are the 12th chapters of Romans and 1 Corinthians.

Read the 12th chapter of Romans and the 12th chapter of 1 Corinthians.

Q4. List the spiritual gifts found in Romans 12 and 1 Corinthians 12.

Q5. Into what general categories can the spiritual gifts listed above be grouped?

Q6. What is the stated purpose of all spiritual gifts?

Q7. To what is the church being compared and how is this instructive?

Q8. What is the relationship between the comparison addressed by Question #4 above and the use of spiritual gifts?

Q9. How would you synthesize or combine the teaching from the 12th chapter of Romans and the 12th chapter of 1 Corinthians regarding spiritual gifts and their use?

Determining Your Ministry Identity

You may be asking, "How can I determine my ministry identity?" The following paragraphs present the fourfold answer to this question.

By Prayer

Your ministry identity corresponds to the "good works, which God prepared ahead of time" that you should walk in them. This being the case, I can guarantee that He is eager to reveal those good works to you, provided you are eager to obey Him when He does. Moreover, James 1:5-8 asserts that God is eager to give us wisdom to discern His will, provided we ask in faith.

By Experiment

Your ministry identity corresponds to works of ministry that you can do well; in other words, it corresponds to your sweet spot, to adopt a metaphor from the game of tennis. Why? Because you are God's work of art, and He specifically and intentionally designed you so that you can perform within your ministry identity with great power and fruitfulness. Therefore, be willing to expose yourself to various areas of ministry: administration, service, preaching, teaching, evangelism, mercy, or encouragement. In this way, God may reveal areas of giftedness that you might never have considered.

A ministry leader, such as a lead pastor, often falls prey to the **tyranny of the urgent** – such as administrative tasks that were due yesterday, or even last week. This is especially true in the case of a small church which cannot afford a large paid staff. As a result, the leader is forced to devote a sizeable percentage of his time and energy performing tasks which others could perform and which lie outside of his sweet spot. If this situation continues for extended periods of time, the leader is likely to experience burnout and may be motivated to resign his position. The remedy is for the leader to strenuously and proactively resist the tyranny of the urgent by surrounding himself with people whose ministry identities complement his own and to whom he can delegate significant responsibilities. The general rule of thumb is each ministry leader should be operating within his sweet spot at least 65% of the time for greatest effectiveness, both individually and collectively.

By Enjoyment

A corollary to the ministry identity corresponding to tasks that can be performed with great power and fruitfulness is it corresponds also to tasks that are enjoyable. When we are operating within the sphere of our ministry identity, we actually feel energized as opposed to drained.

Colossians 3:23-24. Whatever you do, do it enthusiastically, as something done for the Lord and not for men, knowing that you will receive the reward of an inheritance from the Lord. You serve the Lord Christ.

Q10. What is the application of this passage to operating within the sphere of our ministry identity?

Notes & Reflections

Chapter 7. The Clergy/Laity Dichotomy

What do I mean by the term clergy / laity dichotomy? It is the concept that in a local community of faith the paid pastoral staff members are the clergy, and they perform virtually all the work of the ministry. The members of their congregation are the laity; their function is to contribute financially to the support of the pastoral staff, but for the most part they are relatively passive consumers of the ministerial output of the pastoral staff. When and from what source did this concept originate?

Origin of the Clergy / Laity Dichotomy

In order for you to understand the origin of the clergy / laity dichotomy, I need to briefly sketch the early history of the Christian church. The Patristic Period of church history refers to the period of 100 – 500 AD – that is, the time of the Church Fathers, which began after the death of the original apostles and continued until the time the Western Roman Empire began to crumble due to the combination of internal corruption and barbarian invasions. During this entire period, there was a single, integrated, ecumenical Christian Church. The church was led by a collection of bishops, each of whom was responsible for the churches in a geographical region. Also, during this entire period, Rome was the capital of the Roman Empire.

Constantine became emperor in the early 4th century AD. Responding to what he claimed was a vision from God, he established Christianity as the religion of the empire. It is no surprise that this move precipitated an enormous surge in the number of people who professed to be Christians, and who therefore wanted to become members of Christian churches. How would the bishops of the church care for a burgeoning number of people flocking into their churches?

Before the time of Constantine, the Christian church had been buffeted by persecution, and therefore its members were, for the most part, serious disciples who were well established in their faith. However, after Constantine, the pressure of persecution was removed, and the huge influx of new converts from paganism were not well established in their faith. In fact, many of them – perhaps a majority – were what I have labeled as nominal Christians – Christians in name only, CINOs.

The radically shifting demographics of the church posed a serious problem to the bishops, and the pressures created by the shifting demographics brought about a migration toward the clergy / laity dichotomy whereby little if any ministry work was expected from the laity. Their function was to attend the services of the church, receive the teaching and other ministry provided by the clergy, and of course, financially support the clergy. This situation prevailed from the waning years of the Patristic Period, through the Medieval Period which followed, and into the Reformation Period, which began in the first half of the 16th century. In all fairness, the Reformers endeavored to restore the biblical function of the laity. However, despite their efforts, the clergy / laity dichotomy persists even into the 21st century, especially in the case of the Roman Catholic Church, the Eastern Orthodox Church, and the so-called mainline Protestant denominations.

Now it is time for us to critically evaluate the clergy / laity dichotomy. In the previous Session we have already studied the Scripture passages that provide a basis for our critical analysis.

Q1. Is the clergy / laity dichotomy a biblical concept? Explain your answer based up Scripture.

Q2. Based upon the Scripture passages we studied in Session 6 regarding ministry identity, identify the leadership gifts that God has given to the church.

Q3. What is the function of those with leadership gifts with respect to the overall goal of building up the body of Christ?

Q4. What group of people is responsible for doing the work of ministry?

Q5. What is the impact of the clergy / laity dichotomy on the concept and practice of ministry identity?

Christ is the head of His church, which He is carefully constructing for the purpose of functioning as His body and doing His work in the world. Just as each member of a body has a particular function, so each individual Christ-follower has a specific role within the body of Christ, which is the church. To equip each one for this function or work, which is certainly essential to the healthy and effective functioning of the whole, Christ has dispensed leadership and ministry gifts. As the people in a local assembly of disciples mature in the practice of their leadership and ministry gifts, the whole church grows and matures into greater fruitfulness.

Discovering one's ministry identity is crucial to fulfilling his unique function in building up the church as the body of Christ. A danger to be avoided, however, is an overly rigid definition of that identity. Christ may confer upon us leadership or ministry gifts that are needed to meet a particular need in the church at a particular time. It is important to be sensitive to God's leading and exhibit a willingness to be used of Him in whatever manner He sees fit.

Q6. Have you ever experienced a call of God into a ministry you considered outside of your ministry identity? How did you respond and what was the outcome?

Notes & Reflections

Chapter 8. Walking in the Spirit

Introduction

Figure 2 in Session 2 portrays the tripartite human personality in right relationship with the Triune God.

> *To walk in the Spirit means that I am walking in the way determined by the Spirit. I am constantly subject to His authority, and I am habitually moving in accordance with His direction.*

In this session, we shall endeavor to define from Scripture practical principles for walking in the Spirit.

In order to grow in the seven virtues listed by the Apostle Peter in 2 Peter 1:3-11 and discussed in Sessions 2 through 5, it is essential that we master the art of living and walking in the Spirit instead of in the flesh. For the personality of Christ to shine through our own personality, a genuine spiritual transformation is required.

It is not possible to accomplish this in the flesh by a sheer strength of the will and discipline. It is only possible through the power of the Spirit at work in our lives as we habitually yield to His authority.

Faith is Key

Recall that Peter's Star, Figure 1, has faith at its center, and from that center all seven of the virtues flow: moral excellence, experiential knowledge, self-control, patient endurance, godliness, brotherly kindness, and self-sacrificing love. The faith at the center of Peter's Star is none other than the faith of Jesus Christ Himself, which is activated in our spirits by the power-packed message about Christ in the hands of the Holy Spirit in accordance with Romans 10:17. It is the faith of Jesus by which we are justified, and it also His faith by which we live.

Galatians 2:15-20. We... know that no one is justified by the works of the law but by the faith of Jesus Christ. And we have believed into Christ Jesus so that we might be justified by the faith of Christ and not by the works of the law, because by the works of the law no human being will be justified... For through the law I have died to the law, so that I might live for God. I have been crucified with Christ and I no longer live, but Christ lives in me. So then, the life I now live in the body, I live by the faith of the Son of God, who loved me and gave Himself for me. [Adapted from the HCSB]

Colossians 2:6-7. Therefore, as you have received Christ Jesus the Lord, walk in Him, rooted and built up in Him and established in the faith, just as you were taught, overflowing with gratitude.

Q1. Both passages quoted above present teaching regarding how we are to walk in the way of Christ and the apostles. Carefully read both passages and then interpret the teaching they contain.

Reflect on the life and ministry of Jesus Christ as recorded in the four Gospels. Clearly, Jesus stands as our perfect model as to how one should go about walking in the Spirit. I recommend your reading through the entire Bible at least once a year so that you can recall from memory how Jesus conducted His life and ministry as well as other key passages and events in the Hebrew scriptures.

Q2. What clues can we glean from the life and ministry of Jesus Christ as to how one should go about walking in the Spirit?

Psalm 32:7-9. You are my hiding place; You protect me from trouble. You surround me with joyful shouts of deliverance. Selah. I will instruct you and show you the way to go; with My eye on you, I will give counsel. Do not be like a horse or mule, without understanding, that must be controlled with bit and bridle or else it will not come near you.

Isaiah 30:21. ... And whenever you turn to the right or to the left, your ears will hear this command behind you: "This is the way. Walk in it."

These are two exemplary passages from the Hebrew Scriptures that present teaching as to how God guides and directs the lives of His children. Hopefully, you can think of others.

Q3. Based upon the teaching presented in the above two passages, plus any others you can identify, summarize the principles of divine guidance set forth in the Hebrew Scriptures. Do you believe these principles are still operative under the new covenant?

Q4. Based upon all the biblical passages you have considered in answering Question #1 through Question #3 above, create a personal checklist of principles for walking in the Spirit.

Read the 8th chapter of Romans and the 5th chapter of Galatians.

Q5. The 8th chapter of Romans and the 5th chapter of Galatians present important teaching concerning the result of walking in the Spirit versus walking in the flesh. List and compare the characteristics of each.

Figures 3 and 4 graphically illustrate the difference between walking in the Spirit and walking in the flesh.

Walking in the flesh involves thinking, speaking, and acting based solely upon the input received from the physical senses, interpreted in accordance with the natural intuition and lived experiences in this world apart from God. No account is taken of what God says or the leading of His Spirit.

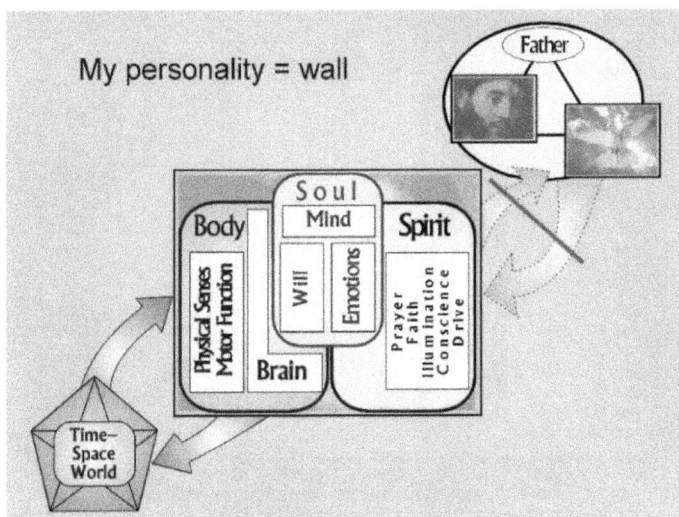

Figure 3. Walking in the Flesh

Living this way is tantamount to living as an atheist. The one who walks in accordance with the flesh is, at least temporarily, living as if God doesn't exist.

The one who is walking in the flesh is preventing the glory of Christ's personality from shining through his personality. As depicted in Figure 4, people around that person observe, through his words and actions, what he is by nature, whether good or bad; they do not observe the glorious personality of Jesus Christ radiating through him.

However, walking in the Spirit is radically different. It begins with the firm conviction that the way in which God's word represents reality is true, especially when it seems to conflict with what can be observed through the physical senses. It involves making decisions based on what Scripture says, even if that goes against how we feel or what circumstances may appear to require.

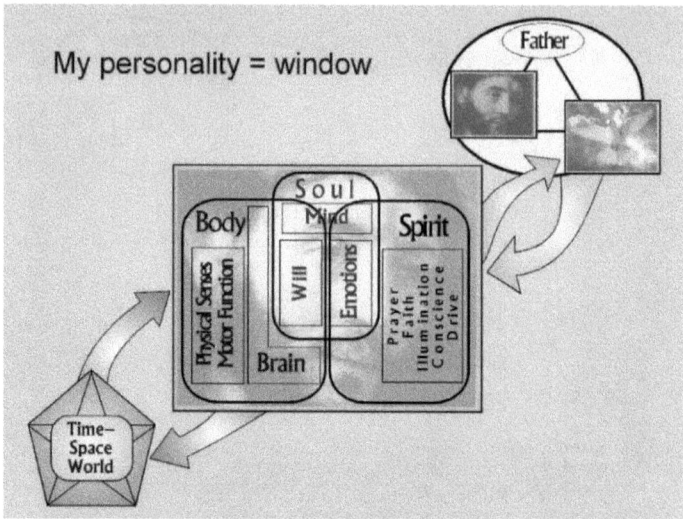

Figure 4. Walking in the Spirit

Walking in the Spirit means that in all circumstances we are governed by the mind of Christ as mediated through the ministry of the Holy Spirit.

The result of our ordering our lives in this way causes us to become windows through which the personality of Christ is seen, rather than walls, obscuring His image.

Q6. Based upon all your studies thus far, list the resources God has furnished that would enable us to walk in the Spirit as described above. (Hint: As a point of departure, check out 2 Peter 1:3-4.)

Read the 7th chapter of Romans

Q7. How would you describe the state of mind and emotions of the person who endeavors to live as a Christian solely through exertion of will and strength of discipline?

Read Hebrews 3:7-4:13.

This is a passage to which we have referred earlier in the WitW study. At this point in our study, I want you to focus upon the connection between faith and rest. Reflect also on the life and ministry of Jesus as represented in the four Gospels. One cannot escape the serenity with which He navigated His life and ministry, often in the face of intense pressure and persecution.

Q8. Discuss the balance between discipline and rest that should characterize the person who is walking in the Spirit.

Now let us consider several scenarios that can arise in the course of life and ministry. For each circumstance, list the appropriate response according to the flesh as well as that according to the spirit. Feel free to include any other circumstances.

For example, in the circumstance of an unexpected ministry challenge, a fleshly response might be anxiety and a feeling of pressure and stress, whereas a spiritual response would be prayer and trust in God's enablement.

- Lack of funds

- Insult or offense

- Injury or sickness

- Marital issues

- Family issues

Challenging circumstances such as those listed above test the validity of our claim to be Christ-followers. In the absence of such challenges, following Christ is comparatively easy.

Notes & Reflections

Chapter 9. Review & Discussion

Displaying Christian Virtues

The necessary fruit of the faith of Jesus Christ is a thrust of the true disciple's life toward Christlikeness, a life that manifests the Christian virtues listed by the Apostle Peter in 2 Peter 1:3-11, and the fruit of the Holy Spirit listed by the Apostle Paul in Galatians 5:22-23. I represented Peter's seven virtues as a seven-pointed star – Peter's Star, Figure 1. At the center of the star is the faith of Jesus Christ; radiating out from that center are moral excellence, experiential knowledge, patient endurance, godliness, brotherly kindness, and self-sacrificing love. We compared Peter's list with that of Paul, who represents the fruit of the Holy Spirit as love, joy, peace, patience, kindness, goodness, faith or faithfulness, gentleness, and self-control.

We concluded that these two lists are complementary; in both cases, the manifestation of the faith of Jesus Christ dwelling within a person is the very personality of Jesus Christ radiating through that person.

The virtues of the Christian life and the fruit of the Holy Spirit are the product of a human personality habitually walking in accordance with the Spirit.

Discovering One's Ministry Identity

I have stated more than once in the WitW study that the salvation procured for us by Jesus Christ at such horrendous cost is not only deliverance from the torments of hell, as important as that may be. More than that, it is deliverance into a distinctive ministry identity, which corresponds to a unique combination of talents, life experiences, and enablements specifically conferred by the Holy Spirit. This unique combination equips us to function with great power and fruitfulness in a ministry arena that corresponds to our

63

ministry identity. The purpose of the ministry identity is to contribute to the building up of the body of Christ.

While some people may possess very visible gifts, such as preaching or teaching, the body of Christ cannot function properly unless all His disciples are participating in the work of Christ and His church through the exercise of their unique spiritual gifts. Gifts of helps, mercy, and administration are equally necessary to those of preaching, teaching, and evangelism.

The way to discovering our ministry identity often entails participating in various ministries on an experimental basis to assess performance, personal enjoyment, and fruitfulness according to the testimony of those receiving our ministry. God has so designed us that our ministry identity corresponds to those ministries in which we perform well, enjoy, and in which we are fruitful.

The affirmation of the Holy Spirit and other believers should confirm our ministry identity. Serving in the "sweet spot" of our ministry identity brings great pleasure, satisfaction, and a sense of being used by the Lord in His work.

Learning to Walk in the Spirit

It is impossible to manifest the Christian virtues identified by Peter, to produce the fruit of the Spirit listed by Paul, or to succeed in doing the work of ministry according to our ministry identity apart from the supernatural work of the Holy Spirit in our lives.

John 15:5. I am the vine; you are the branches. The one who remains in Me and I in him produces much fruit, because you can do nothing without Me.

Walking in the Spirit is the key to success in all aspects of Christian life and ministry. Apart from the Spirit, we can do nothing that is pleasing to our Heavenly Father.

At the very beginning of the WitW study, we came to recognize that way in Scripture is a technical term for pattern of conduct or lifestyle. Corresponding to this, **walk** in Scripture is a technical term for executing a pattern of conduct or lifestyle. And so, **walking in the Spirit** is a technical term for thinking, speaking, and acting in accordance with the moment by moment direction of the Holy Spirit.

God allows us the freedom to choose between walking in the flesh or walking in the Spirit. Whenever we walk in the flesh, people around us see the flesh – the good along with the bad and ugly. Whenever we walk in the Spirit, people around us see the glorious personality of Jesus Christ radiating through our personalities. **The choice is between window or wall, as portrayed in Figures 3 and 4.**

According to the testimony of the Apostle Paul in the 7th chapter of Romans, attempting to walk in the way of Christ and the apostles out from the energy of the flesh leads to utter frustration, abject despair, and, ultimately, death. In contrast, walking in the way of Christ and the apostles by the continuous enablement of the Holy Spirit leads to joy, peace, and, ultimately, eternal life.

Discussion Questions

Q1. Discuss the significance of the ordering of the seven virtues of the Christian life in accordance with 2 Peter 1:3-11 and as portrayed in Peter's Star, Figure 1.

Q2. As a result of your interacting with the members of your discussion group over the course of the WitW study up to this point, they should have gained some sense of your ministry identity. Express to them what you think your ministry identity is and ask the group to either affirm it or suggest that you look in a different direction. Summarize their response in the space below.

Q3. Evaluate the percentage of your ministry time that is devoted to your sweet spot.

Q4. What is the power behind your Christian growth and ministry? What energizes you in your ministry and fills you with joy and peace?

Q5. Discuss what is meant by walking in the Spirit and crucifying the flesh according to the Apostle Paul in the 5th chapter of Galatians.

Notes & Reflections

Congratulations on completing Book 9. You are now ready to move onto Book 10, Disciplines of the Kingdom.

Afterword

About Us

WitW is a product of Daystar Institute of Biblical Theology and Leadership Development (DI), which is dedicated to supporting local churches in fulfillment of their mission of making disciples of all nations. We have two offices: DI / NM is based in Albuquerque, New Mexico, and DI / A is based in Kampala, Uganda. Please do not hesitate to contact us at www.DaystarInstitute/NM.us if you have any questions or comments or wish to request training in the use of our materials.

Peter Briggs is founder and president-emeritus of Daystar Institute of Biblical Theology & Leadership Development. In addition to teaching and mentoring, Dr. Briggs has authored the WitW Study Guide Series to challenge students in uncompromising discipleship, practical Christian theology, and building a biblical worldview. The WitW study has had a great impact in both East Africa and the USA and is an excellent tool for encouraging and equipping disciples of Jesus to actually live out their faith.

Dedication

The *Walking in the Way of Christ & the Apostles Study Guide Series* is dedicated to Reverend Morris Wanje, whose prayers for God to raise up a means for strengthening and equipping young pastors and church leaders in East Africa caused the Holy Spirit of God to move upon the hearts of godly men and women at Daystar Institute/NM to create this study.

Acknowledgments

I am grateful for the heroic efforts of our team of contributors, editors, board of directors, and all who have had a part in the development of the WitW study. In particular, I extend my heartfelt gratitude to my wife, Rosemarie, our daughter, Ruthanne Hamrick, and ministry associates John & Marcie Kinzer, Stephen Patterson, and Michael & Antoninah Mutinda, for their valuable input and help with the Study Guide Series; and to Darienne Dumas and Emily Fuller for proof-reading the texts.

Testimonials

"The *Walking in the Way of Christ & the Apostles* (WitW) series by Dr. Peter Briggs is a powerful tool for fulfilling Jesus' universal mandate to make disciples. WitW is theologically sound, conceptually brilliant, and life- changing for those who are trained by it. The impact of WitW is not only personal transformation into the image of Christ, but also a profound influence on families, churches, and the larger culture, whether in America or Africa or anywhere else. Peter Briggs is a theologian of substantial import, but he has not merely plied his theological craft in the halls of academia. With God's enablement, he has managed to translate biblical truth and disciple-making principles into something that actually works in the real world! Those who embrace and employ *Walking in the Way* in their own lives will find themselves part of a movement affecting generations to come."

Steven Collins, PhD, Executive Dean, Trinity Southwest University

"*Walking in the Way of Christ & the Apostles* (WitW) is a magnificent literary work in biblical theology that offers the student an education in practical Christianity. The WitW study was first introduced in November 2011; since that time we have been using it to instruct ministry leaders and rural pastors at a low cost, and the transformation

70

of lives is phenomenal. Learners get to understand the message of the Bible and are able to study it effectively. In my own interaction with the material since 2012, I have come to realize that Jesus Christ is using it to revive His remnant in Kenya and other parts of Africa, teaching us how to think in a biblical way and be successful in all spheres of life. I am convinced that the WitW material holds the key to Africa's revival, and, in Yahweh's hand, it is a mighty tool for returning the continent back to Him."

Michael Mutinda, Team Leader, Daystar Institute / Africa

Walking in the Way of Christ & the Apostles
Study Guide Series

Part 1: Foundational Principles. These principles are foundational to equip the Christ-follower to have and to be governed by the mind of Christ.

1. The Way of God
2. The Storyline of the Bible
3. Biblical Reality
4. Discovering the Meaning of Scripture
5. Torah: The Fountainhead of Wisdom
6. The Two-Part Christian Gospel

Part 2: The Gospel of the Kingdom of God. Here we explore the ways in which the Christian gospel confronts the prideful rebellion of the human heart and exalts Christ as King over all.

7. Authority of the King
8. Called by the King
9. The Meaning of Discipleship
10. Disciplines of the Kingdom
11. Household of the King
12. The Second Coming of the King

Part 3 – The Gospel of God. This final set explores how the Christian gospel affords a complete solution to human depravity and the threefold problem of sin and death.

13. Introduction to the Gospel of God
14. The Reason for the Gospel of God
15. Content of the Gospel of God
16. Perversions of the Gospel of God
17. Application of the Gospel of God

Theological Readers (TR)

TR1 – Part 1: Foundational Principles
TR2 – Part 2: The Gospel of the Kingdom of God
TR3 – Part 3: The Gospel of God
TR4 – Resources and Appendices

Theological Handbooks (TH)

TH1 – Part 1: The Way of God
TH2 – Part 2
TH3 – Part 3

Connect with us at www.DaystarInstituteNM.us, or
Contact us via email at WalkingintheWayUSA@gmail.com

WitW
Walking in the Way of
Christ & the Apostles

www.ingramcontent.com/pod-product-compliance
Lightning Source LLC
Chambersburg PA
CBHW071928020426
42331CB00010B/2775